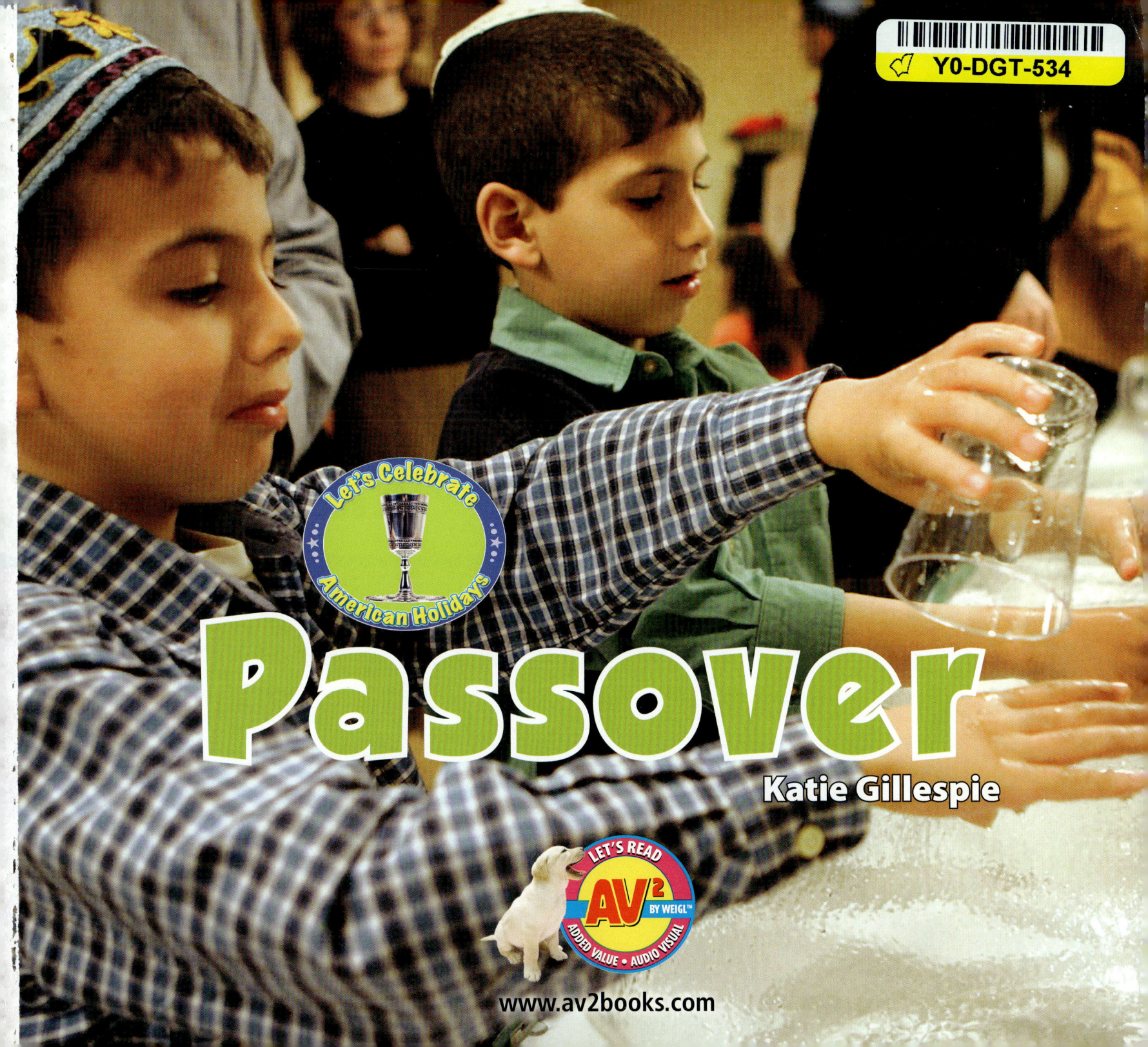

Passover

Katie Gillespie

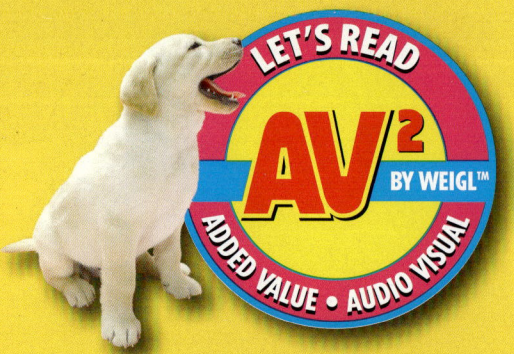

AV² provides enriched content that supplements and complements this book. Weigl's AV² books strive to create inspired learning and engage young minds in a total learning experience.

Your AV² Media Enhanced books come alive with...

 **Audio**
Listen to sections of the book read aloud.

 **Key Words**
Study vocabulary, and complete a matching word activity.

 **Video**
Watch informative video clips.

 **Quizzes**
Test your knowledge.

 **Embedded Weblinks**
Gain additional information for research.

 **Slide Show**
View images and captions, and prepare a presentation.

 **Try This!**
Complete activities and hands-on experiments.

... and much, much more!

Go to www.av2books.com, and enter this book's unique code.

BOOK CODE

U524226

AV² by Weigl brings you media enhanced books that support active learning.

Published by AV² by Weigl
350 5th Avenue, 59th Floor New York, NY 10118
Website: www.av2books.com

Copyright ©2016 AV² by Weigl
All rights reserved. No part of this publication may be reproduced, stored in a retrieval system, or transmitted in any form or by any means, electronic, mechanical, photocopying, recording, or otherwise, without the prior written permission of the publisher.

Library of Congress Control Number: 2015934749

ISBN 978-1-4896-3629-4 (hardcover)
ISBN 978-1-4896-3630-0 (softcover)
ISBN 978-1-4896-3631-7 (single user eBook)
ISBN 978-1-4896-3632-4 (multi-user eBook)

Printed in the United States of America in Brainerd, Minnesota
1 2 3 4 5 6 7 8 9 0 19 18 17 16 15

072015
070715

Editor: Katie Gillespie   Design and Layout: Ana María Vidal

Every reasonable effort has been made to trace ownership and to obtain permission to reprint copyright material. The publisher would be pleased to have any errors or omissions brought to its attention so that they may be corrected in subsequent printings.

Weigl acknowledges Getty Images and iStock as the primary image suppliers for this title.

Let's Celebrate American Holidays

Passover

CONTENTS

2   AV² Book Code
4   When Is Passover?
6   What Is Passover?
8   Matzoh
10 Where We Celebrate
12 Coming Together
14 How We Celebrate
16 More Traditions
18 Mitzvah
20 Special Celebrations
22 Passover Facts
24 Key Words/Log on to www.av2books.com

Passover is celebrated for seven or eight days. It starts on the 15th day of the Hebrew month of Nisan. Passover is a time to remember how the Hebrews were freed from slavery and left Egypt.

Passover falls in the spring each year, around March and April.

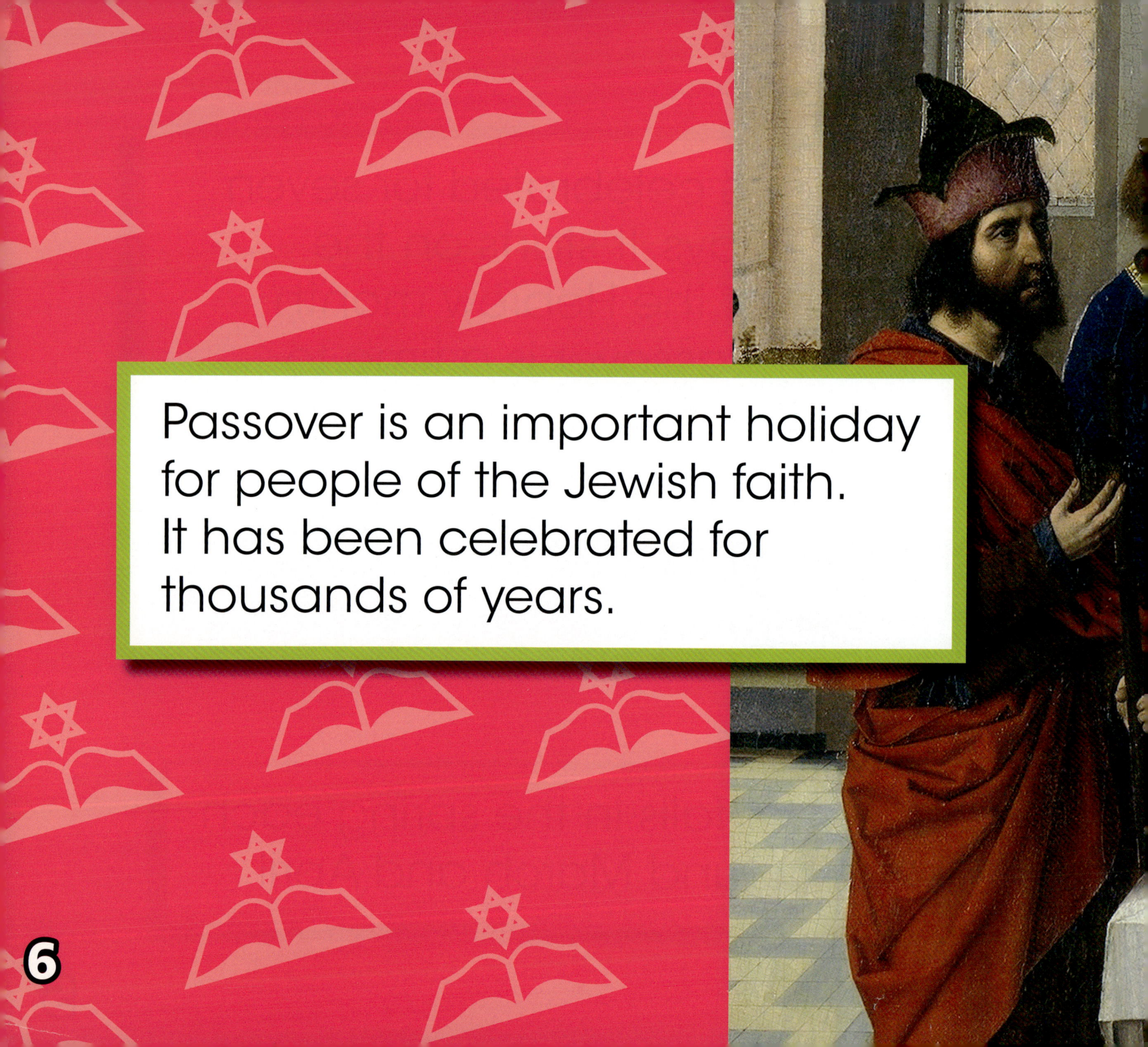

Passover is an important holiday for people of the Jewish faith. It has been celebrated for thousands of years.

7

People eat bread called matzoh during Passover. Matzoh is made from water and flour.

A piece of matzoh is hidden as part of a traditional game.

In ancient times, people went to the Hebrew temple in Jerusalem for Passover. They came together to pray and celebrate.

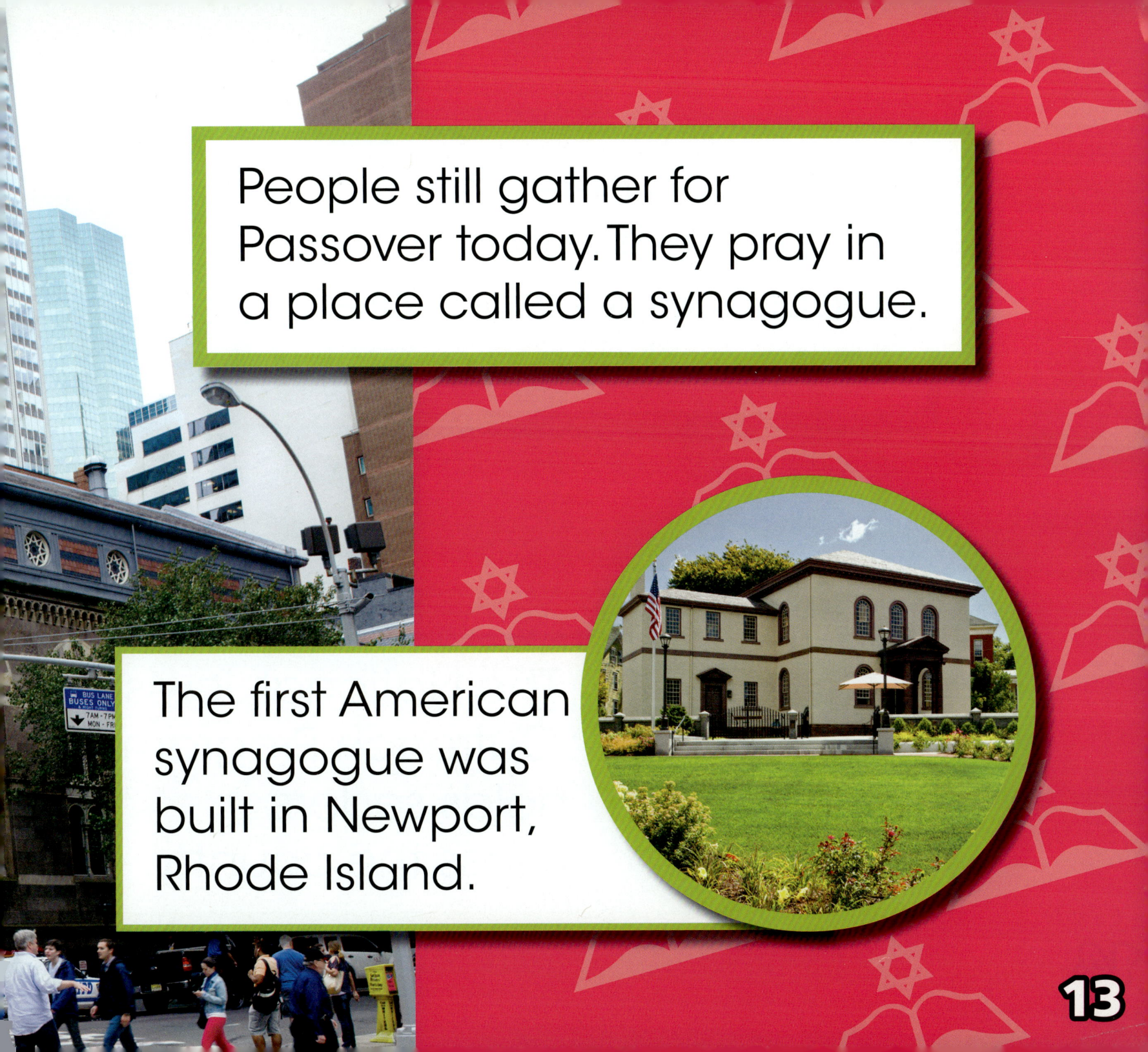

People still gather for Passover today. They pray in a place called a synagogue.

The first American synagogue was built in Newport, Rhode Island.

13

Passover is celebrated with a meal called a seder. Special foods are eaten and stories are told.

The National Jewish Outreach Program holds seders across the country.

Passover is a time to do good deeds. The Hebrew word for a good deed is mitzvah.

19

A book called the Haggadah is read at the seder. It lists the right order to eat each food.

The first English Haggadah was printed in London, England in 1770.

PASSOVER FACTS

These pages provide more detail about the interesting facts found in the book. They are intended to be used by adults as a learning support to help young readers round out their knowledge of each holiday featured in the *Let's Celebrate American Holidays* series.

Pages 4–5

Passover is celebrated for seven or eight days. It is one of three Jewish pilgrimage festivals, along with Shavuot, the Feast of Weeks, and Sukkot, the Feast of Booths. Traditionally, Jewish people were meant to travel to Jerusalem three times a year to celebrate these feasts. Although it is not a federal holiday in the United States, many Jewish businesses and organizations are closed during the week of Passover.

Pages 6–7

Passover is an important holiday for people of the Jewish faith. It is a celebration of the 13th century BC event known as Exodus, the liberation of Jewish slaves from Egypt. It is believed that when God "smote the land of Egypt," he passed over the homes of the Israelites. This is where the term "Passover" comes from. Led by Moses, the people of Israel were free to leave Egypt and pass safely through the Sea of Reeds. This is one of the most significant moments in Jewish history.

Pages 8–9

People eat bread called matzoh during Passover. Matzoh is an unleavened, or yeastless, bread. It is eaten in honor of Exodus. When the Jews left Egypt, they did not have time to wait for bread dough to ferment. This is why unleavened bread is part of the Passover ritual. In fact, Passover is sometimes referred to as the Feast of Unleavened Bread. It is traditional for a piece of matzoh, known as afikomen, to be hidden somewhere in the house. The child who finds it is rewarded with a special gift.

Pages 10–11

In ancient times, people went to the Hebrew temple in Jerusalem for Passover. For thousands of years, the most important parts of the holiday were the removal of yeast and bread from people's homes, and eating a large meal with friends and family. People would attend temple, joining as one large family to pray. A lamb was often brought to the temple as a spring offering. Today, some people still travel to the remains of the Hebrew temple in Jerusalem for Passover.